NIA DAVIES

All fours

ISBN: 978 1 78037 364 5

First published 2017 by
Bloodaxe Books Ltd,
Eastburn,
South Park,
Hexham,
Northumberland NE46 1BS.

www.bloodaxebooks.com
For further information about Bloodaxe titles
please visit our website or write to
the above address for a catalogue.

Supported using public funding by

**ARTS COUNCIL
ENGLAND**

Printed in Great Britain by Bell & Bain Limited, Glasgow, Scotland, on
acid-free paper sourced from mills with FSC chain of custody certification.

ALL FOURS

Nia Davies was born in Sheffield and studied English at the University of Sussex. She has been editor of *Poetry Wales* since 2014 and has worked on several international and collaborative projects such as Literature Across Frontiers, Wales International Poetry Festival and Wales Literature Exchange. Her poems and essays have been published and translated widely and she has appeared in several international festivals. A frequent collaborator with other poets and artists, she co-curated Gelynion, a Welsh Enemies project on collaboration in contemporary poetry in Wales in 2015. Her pamphlets, *Then Spree* (Salt, 2012), *Çekoslovakyalılaştıramadıklarımızdanmısınız or Long Words* (Boiled String/Hafan, 2016) and *England* (Crater, 2017), were followed by her first book-length collection, *All fours* (Bloodaxe Books, 2017). She is undertaking practice-based research at the University of Salford.

CONTENTS

You will never guess my name

11   About me
12   Mossy Coat
14   *'I know descent lives in the word decent'*
15   *'& blow in the god's good wake to leave only pounded dust'*
16   Pantheon
18   With Sinbad
19   *The First Riddle:* Pussy Riddle Dialogue
20   *The Second Riddle:* You will never guess my name
21   *The Third Riddle:* The Underbelly
22   *The Fourth Riddle: no* riddle

Happy Birthday to me

27   Poem with sex
29   psychoanalysis
30   in the year ninety
32   Hello Beautiful
34   Born in a moody basket
36   If you go west

Listen

39   A word in your shell-like
40   Many Tremors
41   'We make an insubstantial territory'
42   Of course he thinks part-mythic

Lemon yellow epithet

45   *the mediums of viktor ullmann*
47   Relations
49   Tiny nudist colony
50   18
52   Dear Diary
54   Let's make an experience

from **Çekoslovakyalılaştıramadıklarımızdanmısınız** *or*
LONG WORDS

57   the hatch a bullet flies out of when exiting a tunnel

58   for your [plural] continued behaviour as if you could not be desecrated

59   for those who were repeatedly unable to pick enough of small wood-sorrels in the past

60   also for those who have turned like counterrevolutionaries

61   about to become the leader of a contemptible palaeontology conservatory

62   the most emotionally disturbing (or upsetting) thing

64   [two] people trying to scatter pretended lies with each other

65   most anticrystalising

66   Are you one of those people whom we couldn't make to be originating from Czechoslovakia

try, for a variety of reasons, a sledgehammer

69   It is not sufficient to be waiting like this

71   things to try before you die

72   nature poem

73   the magical experience

74   I Want To Do Everything

77   ACKNOWLEDGEMENTS

You will never guess my name

for Elizabeth Hamilton Watts

About me

Because I was sleeping all over here,
and here. The magnesium intake nightly,
the slosh of the road in the distance.

Heaven had already soiled me.
Who's that scaling the terraced garden?
I opened one eye in the dark,
then someone braver opened both.

I made to swing out of a lime tree,
said *deepen, foster.* Thought of when I was young,
I would think selkies, think *skerry calf.*

I would listen through lids,
less scathing, less scrape and tangle.
An alarm sounded and everyone ignored it.

Mossy Coat

I wanted to live out of party bags and dream daily in bread-making references. I wanted to write about haunted sties and brown trousers, the look of champagne on your face, the look of *rate-nice/right-nice*.

I would write about sealing practices, I said. I wanted Ermintrude, or any woman by that name, to come to my party.

I thought how I'd like pieces of his muscles to keep for the night, I wouldn't waste them.

And of course I thought about Mossy Coat. She singles out the bad men, the ghosts from the guests, hears Baba Yaga's distant rumble.

I wanted the bad man to come back and fetch me. I wanted a loom as a bed. I said my time with me should be limited. I wanted masochistic dressing-up mode.

I wanted furlongs of him. And pussy was a word I could think about – 'Pussy' 'Cunt' / 'Mossy' 'Coat'. Or maybe a rap on the word 'sundress'.

I couldn't think about 'I' anymore, it was bad for me, so I thought about him all dressed up like a pig-herder or a mountain lion.

And about wedges and my moccasin-together-look with a heel, *Look Pocahontas, Look!* But I wasn't sporting either. Instead I still hadn't put my trousers on.

I just thought about Mossy Coat and how she was a good role model for me. Especially for finding the right man and leaving him with the right shoe. I wanted Baba Yaga to come and eat me up.

I wanted to come over as a nasty piece of work. Especially as a piece of work and also that he'd be shocked at what I'd become.

Personality-wise, I wanted to be a mismatched underwear set. Certainly I was keen to become a burden.

I can't help the way I feel, I said, especially when it comes to spanking. And what would my mother think about what I'd become in the coat she made me out of moss. That fine, magic moss?

I thought about death, and not in a suicidal way, briefly, but regularly.

I have been managing fine by myself, I said to him. I only joke when I say I need you as my butler.

'I know descent lives in the word decent'

Orpheus controlled the whips
himself. And in the *all right*, *hasty*,
he could access the windy sleep
within a sleep. Could turn up on Sinjar
his eyes streaming. Say *i-and-i*,
totally dreadless and still be alight.

Silver birch and sloe gin,
just to be decent to one another,
make a quiet life in the aftermath,
tell memories of future mammies,
future tea and scones.
He may have considered this.
He may have considered turning whip
into harpstring and placing us
in the tale within a tale.
Or to open us up as a precipice
to look down into: *What I could be*
if I could imagine myself
as woman? But it's hard.

When he opened his eyes they were burning,
there was a window into an aftermath.
I take this window to be a ladder; admit
yourself to the decent life.

'& blow in the god's good wake to leave only pounded dust'

When he pressed my cheek,
the vibration he made. Seriously,
how did I not laugh right back

in his ear. But instead,
but instead, the ill-scent
that felt well-won, or worn.
I'd take his army of birds,

his spell-breaking death already in him
pity the mortal killed by women,
pity the shreds of him he became.

I'd take it. Feathers in shreds.
Foretaste tasted like metals,
some sibilance in his last

number of the night. This is a poem
about drowning or a botched rescue,
where the rescuer sings of himself.

Pantheon

Pan

follows you to a wet wall
to pebbledash your hopes,

that you'd at least seen some
green in the silos. Shivered

when you felt intentions
were not good, arched

to let him pass by quietly.
By the sand heap, bloodshot.

And you, going lightly into night,
unbold, near-visible in the concrete

cupula. He harps his rural
dis-idyll, the id's own claw-hand.

Pan

This one was spotted in the black plots,
a living thing on goose down,

fingers in beard. This one was
surely what crinkles in the fist,

was surely the finer thing on from pastoral,
was pictured with a royal

on a ferry for the Hook of Holland.

Pan

Sleet, you gospel of a witch,
by the elm, the arch, the us.

His bread became the sea.
The sea was a lake we stored fish in.

Under the sun, we undered the sun,
we shouldered the sun and became un,
the us in football chants,

the us in all muscular forays,
the rock bottom. Still chiming,

still the chiming.

With Sinbad

He was salty-lip to a fault,
safe until they mentioned the *singularity*
(they mean the *shiny clarity*).

And then they mentioned
dog (they mean *god*) and made great commotion
in the halls, did their hymns and rites.

I said oh *dog* no, he was never about this,
they misunderstood him. But then they
put me to bed like a babe Moses so I can't protest.

Did he talk untidily? Did he howl at his moon
all glottal stops and decrossed Ts?
Did he persevere entirely unbeknown?

He had a stoopy grace, made a rimshot off the island
in a rinky dink barque. We tried to kiss on the parapet.
I tried to play my sophisticated ailment.

The band played diggy diggy.
We had to row out farther and farther, knew
when I died he'd have to come with me.

The First Riddle

Pussy Riddle Dialogue

What is slaked, is foreplayed in patterns?
The crux

What capsizes capital?
Hands, cunt

What goes three ways?
A Woman

What goes three ways?
A Man

What laughs tears?
The insides of us three

What is more open than ever before?
Universe and its non-universal self

What stinks to high heaven?
Low heaven and its lovely sauce

What is rapture?
art, sourced by heaven

What scales does the voice know?
All of our voices

What is the mower we call destruction?
Obliviousness and its employee

What is the kismet of this riddle?
Fine deliverance, the end

The Second Riddle

You will never guess my name

Call me javelin. A mannequin for spears.
Call me Harriet, if you like. I am
scissor-real. A jar of pickles.
Call me Andrew Happenstance, lovely Xerox.
Lovely evaporation. My biggest concern is
this here riddle told on the cusp, by a makeover
guru such as myself. Call me Evermore, Grecian burn,
Leaf-o-grass. Categorise me under Peckham.
Under Pazartesi (the day after market).
Vasilisa's skull-stick. Stand in the throne hall
and say my name: Miss Never-again,
Miss Happy Harpy (née Julia).
Call me mythic – I'm a toss-up between
'project' and 'ongoing'. I'm nil-by-gusset,
I am tall-boy. Poppy, or die. Seaweed, or die.
St Tropez? It was a place once
and I called it home, soft-nuts.
Soft-gusset. Soft mushroom collar with a triple pleat.
Call me fuckwit, fuck all of it.
Categorise my role alongside soup-kitchen.
Milkweed – why? Flower market – why?
Testes – why? Does everything pointy
have to be phallic? My fame runs, and you'll drum
this in until you're drummed in,
my name, as it is. Remember it.

The Underbelly

Four dangling holes,
four teats, four sweet brothers.
The earth's magnified tonight.
It's laminate, humming at
udder-muscle frequency.
We came from lion's eye and
ride away like night giants.
Four suckling things – a terrace
of creatures, a helm,
a hand in a uterus.
We're purchased buttons
and spilled sprats. We're
like you – any way you
want us. We leak ghost spit.
Purple borage bruise. Hard or heavenly
bread or scooped out manna,
it all comes from us.
Where is the sun I never see?
We live in a chandlery on the face of things
and then we slump in sweat.

The Fourth Riddle

no riddle

not bare not broken
not broken bracket,
no blanket, it is not not
like the sea not like
the distant lights
sensational double knot
hot white my eyelid. / not
mine no palace to shake birds
towards no birdhide
later will realise the sum of no
limbs, feet. / is no nothing
ventured, ad hoc best of times
worst of knock down john
one skin one head two necks,
dissembled blanket. / there
is nothing underneath,
but the righteous brigade
got your back. / now what you
going to do? / no personal lick
didn't squirm in my car seat like the sea
interchangeable nouns. / no none
the dust has barely settled but nothing happens here
arrangement of runic
letters and they spell cock
or foreskin. / maybe that's enough
you couldn't sing your way out of this riddle
oh he def. handles himself well
for an invertebrate. /
oh, help my poem has no meaning
or back bone. / whatever flush chaps say
that's the answer. / no fashion
no grab, cash back
scholars may guess from the Turkish letter ğ

yumuşak g – no sound but its function
its function – ah ah
hold open your mouth
oğ oğ oğ

Happy Birthday to me

Poem with sex

sex is not a project

SUSAN SONTAG

sex as a universal human baseline
sex as solid, rockable
sex as the species' in-joke
sex as the one becalmer, the mashing thing
the underside of sex topples and I share a space with this thought

sex as the great destroyer and creator
as the opposite of death drive
the ex libris of sex is a palm with a word or a letter on it
i search 'piano' and 'open' on Pinterest
sex is happening even when you think it isn't

i like Tamara's piano and that's not a metaphor
desire as inextinguishable smoulder and chief cliché
the notion of so much sex as taunting
vs not living because of sex
the door opens automatically
the word 'romantic' has returned

what does love without sex
have in common with sex without love?
for the past ten minutes I have not been thinking
about sex except to write this
the weather of sex is not only notional
the humidity & restraint
the flicker & boom
the rules of its own time & its knife edge
it's for you to enjoy but it's not
like butter biscuits or stacked books,
a closet full of good quality garments

sex as the open sesame
sexual fantasy as trolling of the self and auto-relief
eros-plasticity of the self and card games
on trains with vodka and sweat
this was not a planned sex this was cod love
dunno it's like a stick-o-rock on the beach

and that has nothing to do with our sex life
sex is rocking the ocean liner and leaving
itself at high tide everywhere,
the shamey side of things,
we don't know how to feel
about your arousal at embarrassment

it's not common to give one's parents
a commentary of one's sex life
in the anechoic chamber of the word 'perfect
love' – sandwiches and crisps
love is not really a buttonhole or a mouse
but I'm sure comparisons have been made

we've come to define ourselves
against others and a mint cocktail
and contrary to what is assumed
woman is not in charge of all breeding
the cheek offered is separate and fulsome
shiny still from crying

I should've cried more in the attic room
it was so bright with moths and rugs
but this was not a good place to lie
down in and I could've chosen better linen
but we didn't have a maid
and what is source, anyhow, the source is
dying

psychoanalysis

the ghost of *best foot forwards*
the ghost of *terribly louche*
something went down and it did not touch the sides
it was poorly and sentimental
as in speaking to the ceiling
as in duplicitous conversation
whereby one person tests another without consent,
whereby a personality presents without a filter on
it's a challenge to get the alter ego into a mackintosh
it's a challenge and the presenter says 'don't give up!'
and that's entertainment, roads wet
and they look like rivers from the bridge,
lightweight, like me,
one of the herd had a bad purpose, like me,
so we set about it
like custard round crumble
so we looked at the ceiling and said the lightning is swell
I don't do badly, especially when I unpeg myself a notch
I don't do too badly, especially when I step out lanternwise
and now the ghost of undervalued people
and now the ghost of their feelings

in the year ninety

there was an angle
      to our gravity-sprint

      steep
      the terraces were pitched
life came out best on telly

& we found out
the meaning of
      vhs
      a loop in the wind
maggie maggie maggie

split concrete
          victorian desks

the bribes were good &
don't put your head in a plastic bag

we knew about saddam and maggy
          and out out out
and oi,
we say no
to texaco,

the petrol blooms   desert spooled through with black smoke

like our own sandstone flushed black
& the stained soil
      in the field we called the park

we were for texaco
          but
we weren't for the war

or for the flu so lurid it woke us in the gloom crying
          legions, legions

and I don't like maggie either
          and I'm against the war

we stuck a rose in our window – out out out

          there was a wall on the telly you could kick down
          and a baby in our own wall
so on its way
          we just couldn't wait

Hello beautiful

how is our symbiosis, our stutter?
Look at me calling over to you.
I'm made of signs and fast-forwards.
I'm lending you my ear. And cheek.

Did you ever even have a stomping ground?
Tell me how that was possible. Even minutely.
We can talk, I can take pictures of you
at the fruit machine. Your clavicles wonder me
        in that glow.

*

Hello beautiful. Science is a bitch. It takes so long to prove
anything. It takes and it takes. Can you believe
me that I am nothing but your other insider.
Nothing if not yours. Your other half (life)
and I've bought you a juicer.

*

Dear beautiful. Head yourself on my lap.
        Heave over here
to my saucer. In the forest
there are rarities. And clearings I've seen from above.
Don't worry yourself with lures. You can be
Vasilisa, Red Riding Hood. You'll find me here,
wolf and witch.

*

Dear delight, I am curried and cusp. I am litres
of sea water, selfish, as you know. Grand light
in the bay. And there are partial bites on your skin.
I am nothing if not a defender of you.

How can one subsist on
barley alone? How can one hope to live at all?

I keep saying Little Miss, like it really is something.
I keep preserving these lemons,
hoping you will one day try them.

*

Dear Beautiful. Remember me?
I am waiting to be your thin thing,
I am already your insides. I am already
a firm believer.

Born in a moody basket

Run-off rain soaks patches
on my coat and trousers. The inner ear
sluicing as dishwater, its commentary:
rest or reprieve yourself, move to make sense.

~

Look up. Berries suspended in thorns
are that same rackety churlish:
an overspill of fluster,
my lurching, a leach of sagey green,

a basketry of moods and nerves
and stomach enzymes caving in on themselves.

~

Beg leave of this carvery of angles,
it says. But where I tend to put my skeleton
at night is the same place I shake myself awake.
Going nowhere. Look to your surplus air.

~

A magnum fizz-spray – ebullience – at the race's end.
As opposed to a quiet bobbing on a slated sea.
As opposed to acts of matter – good deeds.
Be slick of skin. Which is it to be?

~

Some ill-thatched theorems block
each other's light. *Decide,*
choice is a parallelogram,
best made on the slant.

~

Bubbles shrug and rush the glass: ale
and another sun-end is topped off,
wasted, now what of the frecklier sky?

What next in my fidgety solstice?
Heart in the headland — observe the invisible wealth.

If you go west

you will eventually, undoubtedly find shore. We travel and travel, sleep in the dunes, dine under bridges. You keep your thimble-shaped nightlamp close. You store so many berries in my tin cup. Fountainous hunger, unprofessional foraging. Hold on, you tell me, hold on to our plain talk, wheels on the cinder, knuckle rocks for tent pegs. But summer is such a drag on us bones. I can smell the resin unscrubbed from my face. I sing 'happy birthday to me', sweet melting-hot land. Or sweet sea, when it comes out of the haze, the interior smoking behind us.

Listen

A word in your shell-like

Bed-worn, tied to the auricle
pull of strange flowers, something sails:
green beads on a black background,
scurrilous shapes. Marvel-vine,
cave-dwelling hallucinations.
We doze in the old kind of nourished.

Then there is your farcey nature.
Some think you are averse
to the neutral catch-all
of spring, rivers, such things.
I say summer is all honey-hive on our cliff,
and that the seals of the Black Sea are different.

And what about my intertragic notch?
Do you love so? I love so. Purring wonders
come out of you spoon-eared. Wonton soup
is delivered, so tragic, as to be intertragic.
Old soft lobes, you really test me.

Many tremors

do not a woman make. To rectify this, think: radio caverns.
I'd like to sit in my radio cavern and say:
'Could we axe that diver-eared song of muffle-head?'
Let that echo around a little.

Say: 'Let's get ready for your rumble.'
Then put on clothes to make me less of a tremor.
Peter Rabbit fluff socks, cotton pants.
Krasznahorkai's name inside me as an incantation.

Vortex-style overcoat, Wellington boots.
Sasquatch hand-gear. Pre-heated pillbox hat.
Then I'd leave the cavern for a cigarette break.
Take to saying umph 'French Style',

counting my blessings etc,
snowballing myself. Come back in
and play holy moly mother of dogs:
the one you love. Play 'six feet under' by The Unchainables.

Do my disc jockey whirl. Channel the dead
saxophonists of this world
and the last. Say:
'Thank fuck for the voice of the dog.'

As a DJ I'd be styled on hot tamales,
I'd do lashings of sauerkraut.
I'd be Mountain Number 1.
In the mouth of a whale-shaped rock,

I'd indulge my spidery friends, have a yellowed
snacking selection to hand.
I'd be a good icon. Long rid of tremolo.

'We make an insubstantial territory'

partly heaven, partly city-state
partly ether, partly ammonite

being as calm as one can when
steam kisses necks

being as separate as money
is to mildew

money running
through cells

try doing it lying down
try singing it sweetly as maple

try 'calmly elaborate',
same solitude as I. try

fucking whilst whistling,
partly try fucking on an ebb

try dressing up harshly
each murmur and murmette presses

when a letter would suffice
or a seagull as they used to

Of course he thinks part mythic

and of the bell, as it if it were installed
between his ears

and of the abbey, where they, gatherers of temperaments,
are closely knit, are sand dune sound.

The peal, deep, wakes him. *Think
sweet thought, sweet garnish.*

Wakes him full. Summer is awkward,
is the boy in the rowboat. *Think
swallow, sweet arrow.*

Notice, if god is noticeable, among fronds.
If he could make bread made from beachy soil.

How do you install a bell? Swing on it.
Then inside his eyelet, toothlet, gimlet –
mechanics of an 'oh'.

Lemon-yellow epithet

the mediums of viktor ullmann

all the panna cotta and   ribbons
so why be so ang
gry?   he says our hands are busted
ferris wheel and i am
ventriloquising him.   that's an accusation.

I do telly-side professional   bitching.
but you can pet me   while my pelt is warm.
got myself a grilling   on the internet.
while Nathalia Romanenko did his   no.25,
keep going   keep go   ing

my morris minor ankles do   nothing
for me   in   desert boots   too chill
and I feel pretty futile   he even made
    posthumous tweaks   it's 1975
and he's invited   back,
makes harp harpsi   chord.

it's as if he was alive   all   along!
was only hiding in the   furthest chamber.
blancmange   was on my mind
to buffer and stuff   me from any painful thought

or stench   − deathcamp −
mediate all day   and nobody thanks me for it
he made love all of the day & no one thanked him for it.

knew the chats with Chopin   were for nothing
he made swallowed sleigh bell   warm.
Nathalia gazing,   curtseying: we are too broken
     bro   ken

to make this work, I
should shout: don't be pessimistic!
don't indulge in the   present.

I keep ice cream for   miracle usage.
I internalise: oh, just be ha   ha
ppy   and move on

In 1974 Victor Ullman's *Der Kaiser von Atlantis oder Die Tod-Verweigerung*
was prepared for its first performance by Kerry Woodward. Woodward made
a number of changes to the score based on the a consultation with the spirit-
ualist Rosemary Brown who was well-known for her conversations with dead
composers.

relations

argument (0): wine or something similar

indices here
where I have pointed to him
his navel
love is some power
so that when I'm in the bathroom I miss him

argument (1): some people sit in the street and they are not begging!

around 11pm I start to
feel my own uninspired broomhead
limpet muscle
the thingness of my fist, or what's inside

argument (2): just doin' business wid ya!

telling, isn't it,
when you sit still
that racket inside
just goes on unheeded

argument (3): the lumpen effects of clutter

the crowded choosing board
the slow diagonals of the knife
and it seems my osmosis
is different from his

argument (4): the ill way persons speak

personally I've tried
all manner of things suggested
but eventually find

it is I who must open
my mouth and make the sound
of boredom, the kind
induced by a piano lesson.

Tiny Nudist Colony

No wells for bush fires and all these wasps
that hell must hummer with,
       their untimed flight,
       their sacrilegious gold.

       Such heat on the hill, I came down here:
green crook of rock pool,
          spry grass trenches,
          free-thinking animals.

Your fish – in a weedy world – they are yours aren't they?

I am in the business of eating apricots nakedly –
       you see.
All the times I sit here
       I am treating you seedy. Stone stripped from flesh
and dunked in the brine.

Lobsters communicating! Have them.

Dried salted limbs! Take them.

Remembered suddenly my *noswaith dda* attire
my trying taxonomies of sing song

my motionless carriage &/ my empathy carriage

and that I tried to strike the note of clasp-breast horror slasher
    maxed-out body resurrection.

At least tried my best, then.

I can't but pity Exonymic countries
or cobbled together lucky folk, steamy flashes

and Celtic music makes me tired.

I can try and declare myself friendly, but I am
terrible and to be noted,   wind-slapped,

aching pussy, not sure what to want.

In the apples the pips burned.

Stood in the coachyard teleologic,
had a personal jesus on a pin.

        That was something that was passable as sex, at least.
I suppose technicalities made this regrettable.

I have a synthetic lemon feeling about it
the way murderers like it, clean.

Maudlin is not the same as macabre.

Do whatever you like, he says,

and, I, sandalwood,

dream of the threaded lip,
the pursuit of needlework,
bicarbonate of soda citric,

hurt me hurt me
now

hold me hold me
now.

I shouldn't have to explain.

Look at my flaws
all around my life like chickenpox.

Wondered whether I'd die like
this with a cock in my mouth, that's

a flashback, that's why everything has a trigger
warning now, that's when the idea
            full throttle
becomes hundreds of droplets, panic.

We weren't sure if that went well or not,
none of us are sure whether that went well,

when I was 18,
when I was 18 oh god

Dear Diary,

I'd like to cut you up.
Dear Ms Walker, please don't read my diary.

That dream, I told to her on the walk to school.
That dream is a secret.

Dear Diary, we dislike the word buds.
These, they tell us, are the beginning of breasts. Please

spare us the marshmallows over candles
or the teenage pregnancy morality play

with 'Jump around' in, made up by Mr Smith.
I'd like to cut you up and turn you into something new.

Dear Buds, you are fucking awful. Diary,
they told us to be nice and quiet and here are some self defence moves.

We know you can't get pregnant from the foam pit
at Steel City Gym. But we could catch herpes.

Dear diary I am fucking a rabbit.
I'm lying. We hate you, and also we love you.

What we do after school is a secret, diary, I'm lying.
Trip hop is a thing, candles etc.

She doesn't just fancy him,
I love him too but I will never, never tell you how, diary.

They held hands for one week. That was it.
We hold hands all the time.

She was thinking of writing
to that magazine to ask about pads for daily discharge. I was
    thinking how imaginative.

No I wasn't. And I lied about which tapes I like. This week it is
    not Powder. We have mastered blowbacks.

No Henry Firth did not get off with everyone. I.e. I did not and
    never will get off with Henry Firth.

This is not mardiness. I'd like
not to have buds thank you.

I like mild trancy feeling. She likes mild trancy feeling.
We only took poppers once, I'm lying.

Why are we friends? Because of the word Luncheon.
Because of Helen of Troy and Michael Rosen.

Because she had weed. And we both liked competitive reading.
There were some things we both knew.

He made me try a cider lolly. Dear Diary I am revealing it once
and for all, we didn't like *The Hobbit*, we only read it

to get ahead. And the lipstick poem
on the mirror was not us, though I wished it was.

We don't ever get into 'scrapes'.
They are not called 'scrapes'.

Dear Diary I never to listened the Powder tape. But I wanted to.
Fuck off, I'm lying.

Let's make experience

they used to say 'womanish' and that would mean your throw

at St Helen's there are two banks, one enclosure and a grandstand
you'd think this would be clear

let's stroke the surface of Cricket but not get in too deep

bars are colour-coded but I don't think drinks are available

St Helen's the venue is experienced as a separate franchise and is
     not to be confused with St Helen's the grounds

it's cricket season and the students are on Prozac

I know nothing of krill   but I can try to experience it

the leaf-encrustation at Gate A is an experience   and you can
     easily trespass onto the grandstand

ticket sales cannot happen here   if only cricket could attract a
     larger audience

they used to say 'cricket widow' and that would mean bitch

there's a lot of handsome shadows and I feel alienated

I like womanish things like manicures
I'd often be disappointed at the heavy balls

cricket isn't winning around here   it is making nothing happen

Sunday 24th of May at The Cricketers opposite St Helen's: an
     adult party hosted by Mad Jay
(guaranteed an experience)

Yes   let's make this experience cricket   Yes

from

Çekoslovakyalılaştıramadıklarımızdanmısınız *or*
LONG WORDS

the hatch a bullet flies out of when exiting a tunnel

kuulilennuteetunneliluuk (Estonian)

was it a bullet train or a simple bullet
or a bouillon blanc or a second coming
or was it ash wednesday again
over and over or was it exiting somehow on top
or upside the tunnel and what a tunnel
represents is a tunnel but also this other: also passages
and also tubes and pipes and these
things often also refer to women
but men also have pipes and little or large holes
with varying entrances and exits
it's just women get entranced or exited very publicly
often live on the internet
...was it mashed grass on the knees to indicate relinquished virginity
or some other form of debatable purity
or was it a hatch one could open and on the inside you'd find
a baby or some blood or a lost forgotten sperm or
a string for a tampon to exit via
was it something you would cry over
probably not
or was it dried mud dust on the eye
when you recognise you are being bullied
and that makes you a victim of bullying
is that worse in some way?
was it something we could um and ah about forever the hatch of a
        bullet
is it what it is
or what i say it is
as in hurtling?

for your [plural] continued behaviour as if you could not be desecrated

Megszentségteleníthetetlenségeskedéseitekért (Hungarian)

the never-tired
the awl and the augur,
leather pressed through until the light showed
and continued behaviour that
tastes like lighter fluid,
as if not you were not overly sleepless
as if not fortunate and symbolic
as if you could not be desecrated
like all of us other
sacreds, jumping for proper money,
able to read signs that tell what us what indeed
the penury should be like,
we don't have a lens through which to view our behaviour as
others see it
we just have to IMAGINE
and then the good king wenceslas
looked out and i dreamt that man flirted with me till he fell over
    drunk
and i slunk away, skittered in the pool of surplus shiraz,
burnt in the wicker basket set up for such things,
i had another hand to hand just waiting in my pocket
now i have frequent ball aches without the balls to speak of
and such a lot of dripping drool over tooth and gum,
gutted i can't be with you tonight darling
for your awl and augur and your continued behaviours
dear god look upon me kindly with your unknowable unsubstantial
unverifiable looks
and your hot sauce,
bring this desecration back to life.

for those who were repeatedly unable to pick enough of small wood-sorrels in the past

nebeprisikiškiakopūsteliaudavusiems (Lithuanian)

for those of us repeatedly amiss,
for those with ears on fire and
then the heat of the hands-out begging bowl night,
in the past we used ourselves knottily
and burnished overcompensating
bureau-speak, safe-hands in the monetary shallows,
we go unchallenged in ourselves, we forget to look
into those begging bowls deep enough,
there is a waning collective appetite for sorrel,
for early-in-the-year green vegetable mass,
but this hasn't calmed your brutal fish hook hands,
a surplus of mud is also there
we took to asking for burnt greens but not clearly enough,
we got samphire, honey and a terrible hurt
it's just one way to be amiss in this world,
those of us hapless but with enough wood sorrel
did know this once, with our pickings we were mealy and mouth-
     eyed
in the sun-ache we'd be trying to clear woodland hurdles to find
     the sorrel,
we'd try to be small enough to smell it

also for those who have turned like counterrevolutionaries

გაკონტრრევოლუციონერებულებისნაირებისათვისაც (Georgian)

also for those best pleased
with a moniker
a halo uncertain
also in the grave
taste of salsify
a chip off the old collectivised
splitters gurning
on white cream
each wrote a poem entitled 'dad'
carry on childish
a primer
claddings etc
you err on the err
scale of ten to one
scale of [nil]
and wonder, don't wonder

about to become the leader of a contemptible palaeontology conservatory

komencopaleontologiokonservatoriaĉestriĝontajn (Esperanto)

they rob you sideways at the bus stop
after the classic car convention,
yours was always a contemptible rise to fame
and they always had their edifice of cotton,
fossils – like the fossil inside their bodies – and
there are palaeontologists who don't reveal themselves in conversation
who spat upon you
you, pretender to this invented order,
all their tradings off
(is the eel's heart needle-shaped?)
they put their fists in rock cavities
hunch over the mineral dishes
snap each other's jaws shut
with metronome clicks
have wasted years of mineral wealth,
about to become a revolution,
about to dress sensibly for warfare
(if we were in North Korea, we'd have been executed by now)

the most emotionally disturbing (or upsetting) thing
Pinakanakapagpapabagabag-damdamin (Tagalog)

is qualified by an inserted parenthesis,
there is of course a difference between disturbing and upsetting
but that is registered fairly deeply in the person saying the words,
i found the novel *2666* really quite disturbing
i woke up in the night realising it was all real
all those women and girls really did die in ciudad juárez
and are still dying,
in britain a woman dies pretty much every 3 or 4 days at the hand
    of a man
and why i was so disturbed by a book
and not so disturbed by similar statistics from my own island
says something
surely about me or books or whatever it doesn't matter as much as
a girl i went to school with, natalie, who was beaten to death by a
    boyfriend
(he will be coming out of prison quite soon)
it is certainly upsetting that he had already been charged with
    assaulting
a previous girlfriend prior to murdering my classmate
that girlfriend was pregnant at the time he attacked her,
it's those cases, of assault, rape, harassment, psychological torment,
    etc, which hardly ever get much justice
because evidence seems to be a massive problem in these cases,
whereas when the woman is dead
well that's quite enough evidence
i suppose that's the difference between here and mexico
in ciudad juárez a dead woman is perhaps not enough evidence to
    find and jail the killer,
according to *2666* that is,
i woke up in the night knowing i had been thoroughly disturbed
    by *2666*
i told sean to read the book and he still hasn't reached the part
    about the killings,
of course i feel bad that he is about to be disturbed

but in some ways I feel he should be disturbed,
jon gower suggested to me that one reason that part is so effective in
    disturbing a reader is the repetition,
each murder is described carefully and dispassionately and after a few
    hundred of these descriptions instead of being desensitised you
    become more sensitive
and in my case more disturbed
i wonder if that was bolaño's intention
there are also various turkish films that have thoroughly disturbed me
and of course actual life events or things that happened to my friends
such as being raped, stalked, or beaten up by a partner which seems
    to happen suspiciously frequently
these things are of course far more disturbing in the long run as they
    have a deeper effect
though i don't tend to contemplate them reflectively like i do with
    films or books
i am too upset at the time
i was upset by being bullied recently by a middle-aged man but not
    really disturbed
if anything it was a positive therapeutic experience
because i could walk away which can't really be said
for my classmate beaten into a coma and then dead from her injuries.

(for Natalie)

[two] people trying to scatter pretended lies with each other
Nakikipagsisinunga-sinungalingan (Tagalog)

a couple living vicariously
beat each other at a tabletop dancing competition
and one more thing
is the competitive movement of twigs in wind
and how later the couple cast across the field to sow
time and time again little pieces of grave
that trip us all up,
if you believe a lie is akin to death,
if you believe death is a lie in the first place
come scatter here and here
lies we tell ourselves daily,
he screams through the keyhole:
i thought you were dead,
and of course she is
she's just moving around his spaces
so he can go on living a lie
living a lie
he once held a conference with her right hand
there was a time he gained happiness via trellis and derby,
he had no badges to speak of
and he drove his sprinter into hell
most days,
on other days he woke from his nightmare in a carpaccio
of unfulfilled wishes, spread gossip amongst himself,
the wind turned over in rumination
or was it ruination?
they passed the part of the hill where potatoes were grown,
there were ridges and in those ridges they decided
it was better to die here scattering,
it is better to lie down now instead of protesting, he said,
you were always a liar

most anticrystallising

najneprekryštalizovávateľnejšievajúcimi (Slovak)

its source mostly forgotten, tiny hexagonal formations, minerals,
of course the palaeontologists
know nothing of real rocks,
they smoke batteries they are so stupid,
they don't even know all the old geology jokes
or what the fossils inside them are really saying,
things like: give me ketamine, give me methamphetamine
and malbec, because they like a good grape,
there are only one or two ways to stop a
palaeontologist from speaking his or her mind:
remind them of their uselessness
and of the fluid we can use to dissipate crystals,
i woke in the night resenting the palaeontologists
even more than normal, woke up wishing for rocks
and also of fossils which are my enemy, always have been,
especially the fossil inside,
wasn't there some way i could stop the bad crystals from
forming in the first place? wasn't there some magic word?
or was it better to let it happen or at least bring forth the inevitable
breakdown so that cleansing fire and all that TOSH and TWADDLE,
could rinse me out from the inside, shift the dirty fossil once and
      for all?

Are you one of those people whom we couldn't make to be originating from Czechoslovakia?

Çekoslovakyalılaştıramadıklarımızdanmısınız (Turkish)

i couldn't make it go away
and then the collective farms emptied
and then the malnutritioned chickens wandering
into festive heaps
devilish uncertainty
i caught a whiff of some kind of origin and
i couldn't wear that origin for myself we tried repeatedly to make you
    all come from somewhere to make myself
come from somewhere,
now i realise i come from the internet,
that's the true origin of all origins anyway,
we tried very hard
and we stood there in a kind of
brown scandalised waving,
the burning issue was there and we had to douse it down
with an inflammable liquid,
it is true that some beers are made in the microwav
to taste vaguely of nuclear winters,
the rest is all anecdote
when bad things happened in the 80s we always had someone to blame
fashion, thatcher, gorgons,
i stood at the keyhole trying to scream the house down
why are you wearing my brown jacket?
and why are you lying about wearing my jacket?
why is it so cold in this collectivised future?

try, for a variety of reasons, a sledgehammer

It is not sufficient to be waiting like this

A cold shoulder of lamb. And when I wheeze
like this you can feel my pollen.

Night-jar hands – I mean that they are cold.

You've been washing in soil again.

And I've become the seventh sea: a waiting child
waiting for a child, waiting for you to be an adult.

The book entitled *Three Ways to MAKE IT*
could be made from any number of perfectly good trees.

The Christmas wreath has not been taken down by us
or anyone else.

You put most latitudes down as *wanting to visit*.

Night-life is a loneliness machine.

I think of the light shifting from pole to pole through the year
        and if you walked
from Arctic to equator, that would be a long walk but a good walk.

Medicinal waiting.

Floral waiting,
born waiting.

Waiting to not be your mother but someone else's.

What would life as a lawnmower be like?
What would life in the grass be like?

I circle the balustrade once to tell you
I am still waiting. A lamb is white because it is so.

But it can also be brown having been cooked so.

There is kitchen conversation and then there is kitchenette conversation.

You can have my travel bag full of adapter plugs. My lungs
have also gathered tacky stickers from all of the

visits and the visitations.
It's possible I have the right kind of night.

But I am rotten when I think straight.

things to try before you die

Mute on, mute off. Too many choices!

Try placing the Coca-Cola in the dark.

Try, for a variety of reasons, a sledgehammer.

Fox + fur + pussy are names I covet for future selves + pets + babes.

I knew always I was born for this.

There, the pest of our luminosity, it tricks us into thinking we are free.

Try arborism, try aquatic culture.

Try celibacy, you will find all the golden hours you wasted in the topiary.

nature poem

The nature is fresh and it is nettles.
All this thing that is flowing freely from
our certified bosoms,

or our candied ligaments.
I forgot what being beautiful is for,
I worry what zeitgeist could lead to.

Death inevitably.
I'd be disappointed in that oak tree anyway had I seen it,
having had it talked up so.

Yes, nature, I am your client
and your clientele.

Actually I've had some pretty haphazard orgasms lately.

There is something repellant in the image
of a man wanking.

A shame for men really,
is someone to blame? It might be porn.
It's not the kind of natural I mean.

I am in the natural woods,
notebook open. I'd die embarrassed

if any poet found me here being
Romantically overbearing.
And here, a midge in my heart.

the magical experience

it ricocheted, because it was coming and that's when I realised the
       pain
up from my gums
to my hamstrings
oh abandon me

I was working a way out round Yes Yes Yes! my story about those
       terrible times
the body is
readily halved
pain is a badge
a window

summaries of god or godlessness don't tend to open oystershells
and I was
no shell
not relatively safe

not accustomed to being dependent on servants, to being unable
       to service my
trollop needs
cancel my subscription
to *Elle Decoration*

I mean to say there was much to tell you all about. Let me rephrase
       that: I was on all fours
bless my husband
he did not see it coming

I refused to go to Coventry, they sent me anyway, I flew a Cossack
       out of my metaphorical window, I
lay drugless
magical

I Want To Do Everything

Bibulous, happy, exploded in the litter
of pomegranate, I want to live long.

And face the glaciers' flume. It's spring,
it's spring in that toothpaste. The winter is game,

asks me to press forward: evenly. Then spree.
The rubble of my room, the follicles pushed up,

flowering envelopes, springs of seed packeted.
What can be chosen amid this?

In the bed we'll live long to bear orang-utans.
And in clusters of eight we'll count them.

Nine might be holy. And it's better
when it's a charmed story.

Peeled wheat at breakfast, blood oranges and March.
Let it be March soon.

ACKNOWLEDGEMENTS

'I know descent lives in the word decent' is a line from 'Cocktails with Orpheus' by Terrance Hayes.

'& blow in the god's good wake to leave only pounded dust' is a line from 'The Death of Orpheus' by Sarah Howe.

'We make an insubstantial territory' is a line from Virginia Woolf's *The Waves*.

'in the year ninety', 'Tiny nudist colony', 'Born in a moody basket' and 'I want to do everything' appeared in the pamphlet *Then spree* (Salt Publishing, 2012).

The poems in the section *Çekoslovakyalılaştıramadıklarımızdanmısınız or LONG WORDS* are taken from a series which originally appeared in a chapbook by Hafan/Boiled String in 2016 under the same name.

Poems also previously appeared in the journals and anthologies *Best Friends Forever* (Emma Press, 2015), *Binders Full of Women('s Poems)* (2013), *Datableed, Glitter is a Gender* (Contraband, 2014), *Kakania anthology* (2015), *Leg Avant: The New Poetry of Cricket* (Crater, 2016), *Lighthouse, The Lonely Crowd, New Welsh Review, Ofi press magazine, Ploughshares, Poetry London, 3AM, Toe Good Poetry, 3AM, The Quietus* and *Wales Arts Review*. Thanks to the editors of these and other publications for featuring these poems. My deepest gratitude also goes to those who supported the making of this book: Tamara Dellutri, Amy Key, Mark Waldron, Roddy Lumsden, Lyndon Davies, Sarah Howe, Zoë Skoulding, Siofra McSherry, Alexandra Büchler, Sioned Puw Rowlands, Eleri Davies, Elizabeth Hamilton Watts, Tim Watts and Sean Edwards-Kearney.